to the World's best

# Mother

edited by Helen Exley

**目EXLEY**
MOUNT KISCO, NEW YORK, US • WATFORD, UK

# mothers are our making

**M**y mother is like the weather and I am just a seed. Without the sun or the rain I would not be able to grow into a flower, healthy and beautiful. Her warmth and love makes me grow. Bigger and bigger.

LING TAI, AGE 11

If we take our mother away, everything crashes down to become broken dreams and fears. Mothers are our making, and if we have a nasty, sarcastic mother we, too, will be like that. If we have a pleasant, happy, generous mother, that is how we turn out.

SARA ROBINSON

No one could ever take her place.

MICHELE BUCHANAN, AGE 10½

all my family naturally go to my mother when wee have any troubles because she is the heart of our home.

MIRTO AZINA, AGE 14

VICTORIA ONSLOW, AGE 6

# What is a mother?
## The handle on my reins,
## the defender of my dreams,
## the cusion when I fall.

GEMMA MORRELL, AGE 12

There is nobody I know like my mother.
My mother is like the earth, full of
goodness and strong.
When I'm asleep my mother lights up the
dark corners and gently wakes me up.
When the day comes hot and stuffy, my
mother cools me like the rain does.

SHAH RAHMAN, AGE 10½

My mother
hates
telling
me off

SIMON
BRAM

Som times
she pretends
not to see
me, when
I behave
very
badly

CAMILLE
FRASER,
AGE 8

SANDRA MADUE
AGE 8

**O**ne nice thing about mothers is they never reproach you if your best is not good enough. If you drop a "best china" plate and it smashes and you are in tears because it is your mother's only plate with lovely decorations, if you did not drop it on purpose and you weren't holding it sloppily when she had told you to be careful, you will always be forgiven.

TONI STONE

**E**ven when she is angry, her eyes are never looking at me angrily. Since the day I remember myself I never saw her looking at my sister or me angrily.

ERICA LLANTOUDES, AGE 17

# I'm a little baddy

If I aggravate my brother she sends me to bed without any food. I keep on thinking I won't do it again, but I keep on doing it.

MORAG, AGE 8

If I was a queen I would give you anything in the world - like me being a good girl.

HAYLY BERNETT

Mothers may nag at you but it's for your own good.

CHRISTOPHER WILLIAMSON, AGE 9

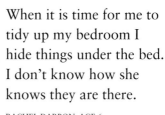

When it is time for me to tidy up my bedroom I hide things under the bed. I don't know how she knows they are there.

RACHEL DARBON, AGE 6

JENNA TURNER, AGE 6

She likes me tho' I can be <u>VERY!</u> naughty but I'm going to be good now Christmas is near!

PAUL WAITE, AGE 10

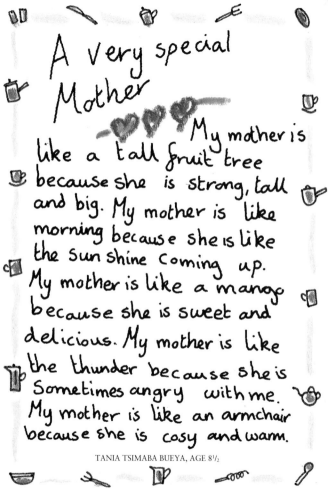

# A very special Mother

My mother is like a tall fruit tree because she is strong, tall and big. My mother is like morning because she is like the sun shine coming up. My mother is like a mango because she is sweet and delicious. My mother is like the thunder because she is sometimes angry with me. My mother is like an armchair because she is cosy and warm.

TANIA TSIMABA BUEYA, AGE 8½

ANTHONY CROUCHER, AGE 8

# Knitting a life

When you knit it is like making a life because you have to be careful in both. Because if you make a mistake when you're knitting you might drop a stitch and leave a hole. And in your life if you make a mistake you might upset your mother and that will leave a hole in your life

MATTHEW CROSS

ANNIE
BLACKADDER,
AGE 4

I think moms
sometimes
are a bit
of an
embarassmen

MALCOLM
HENDERSON,
AGE 8

MELISSA JOHNS,
AGE 6

# funny old things!

**M**xxxx others were sent to the world to nag dads about money to buy dresses for no reason.

VERITY ANNE MOFFAT, AGE 8

She is someone who stops your dad from yelling at you and yells at your dad when he tries to stop her from yelling at you.

DAVID SULLY, AGE 12

My dad got into hysterics over one of my definitions about my mum. Now she won't talk to me for writing it, or to him for laughing at it.

GENEVIEVE, AGE 12

# At her Worst

**M**y mother has the most incredible voice for shouting but mostly for words that can't be printed. I won't go into details.

DANIEL FREEDMAN, AGE 9

Your three worst points are
1. You tell Dad when I'm naughty. I can't think of any more because you're so nice.

MICHELLE DEBOLLA

**M**y mum is really
nice but she is not
nice when she gives
me horrible medicine.

MICHAEL BENNETT, AGE 8¼

# Working hard for us

She works hard for a living and especially for me and my brothers and we all appreciate it. She is really concerned about her family so she works extra hard.

STEPHANIE JONES, AGE 10

While I'm at school my mother is at work, working with all the wordprocessors, and computers. But she's always there at five thirty to give me a loving welcome. It's she who makes the money and she who kisses me goodnight.

ELISHA STANWAY, AGE 10

My mummy teaches managers and she does the washing for me

BEN TIDY

SHARON, AGE 6

DOUGLAS YOUNG,
AGE 5

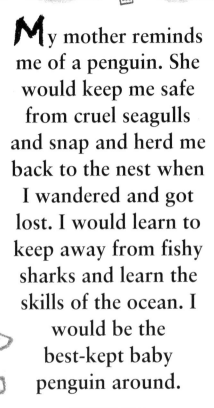

**M**y mother reminds me of a penguin. She would keep me safe from cruel seagulls and snap and herd me back to the nest when I wandered and got lost. I would learn to keep away from fishy sharks and learn the skills of the ocean. I would be the best-kept baby penguin around.

LUCY RYAN, AGE 11

# We're a pair

**W**hen my mother goes somewhere I look for her everywhere. She loves me more than anyone. When I can't find her I cry, I trust her she'll never lie. I can't stay without her. Wherever we walk we're a pair.

HUSNA KHATUN, AGE 11

I like you especially when you are happy. When you are miserable the whole world sinks into the deeps of the ocean.

NICOLA ROBINSON, AGE 7½

Your mother is your best friend

DEAN, AGE 8

RACHEL O'CONNOR, AGE 8

# She loves me

When she buys me presents like hair-bands and taps and a handwriting book, it's telling me that she loves me.

NINA ROBERTS, AGE 7

# THE LOVE STRING

My life is like a long piece of string, full of knots. But my mothers love is another piece of long string, with no tangles no knots. It just runs forever.

LING TAI, AGE 11

PETER WINKLE, AGE 6

# Happy days!

I feel happy and bubbly when Mummy laughs.

SUZANAH OCCARDI

Around her eyes are little laugh lines that come from years of laughing. It is as if someone had ironed out her face but stopped around her eyes for fear of hurting her.

KATRINA PHILLIPS, AGE 12

You make the house a happy place to be
X from Sian X

SIAN FITZPATRICK, AGE 8

PETER McLOUGHLIN,
AGE 8½

The greatest present I've
ever had is your tender,
loving care. And in the
pain you took in having
me. Thank you for the
wonderful life I'm
having and for our
house and home

RYAN GIBBS, AGE 9